Dr. Alicia Holland-Johnson's

Starting and Operating an

ONLINE TUTORING BUSINESS:

*The Blueprint for Running an
Online Learning Organization*

Book Titles by Dr. Holland-Johnson

Dr. Holland-Johnson's
Becoming a Better Tutor:
A Data-Driven Approach to Tutoring

Book 1:
Expanding Your Tutoring Business:
*The Blueprint for Building a
Global Learning Organization*

Book 2:
Expanding Your Tutoring Business:
*The Blueprint for Hiring Tutors and
Independent Contractors*

Book 3:
Dr. Holland-Johnson's
Expanding Your Tutoring Business:
*The Blueprint for Protecting
Your Learning Organization*

Dr. Holland-Johnson's
**Starting and Operating an
Online Tutoring Business:**
*The Blueprint for Running an
Online Learning Organization*

*Note: Check Dr. Holland-Johnson's Personal Website
for her latest work at*
www.drholland-johnson.com

Dr. Alicia Holland-Johnson's

Starting and Operating an
ONLINE TUTORING BUSINESS:

The Blueprint for Running an
Online Learning Organization

Alicia Holland-Johnson, Ed.D

Dedication

This book is dedicated to those who have entered this profession seeking to make a difference in their clients' lives both academically and personally. You are very bold and selfless to share your knowledge with the rest of the world and serve as a merchant of hope to individuals who need help with their learning needs.

Georgia, Amaiya, and future children, this book is also dedicated to each of you and to your future success.

Table of Contents

vii

How this Book is Organized

*D*r. Alicia Holland-Johnson's *Starting and Operating an Online Tutoring Business: The Blueprint for Running an Online Learning Organization* is organized by chapters—the following sections explain what you will find in each chapter.

Chapter 1: Becoming a Legitimate Online Tutoring Company

In Chapter 1, I discuss all of the necessary steps to legitimize your online tutoring company so that you can do business. You will have an opportunity to assess your start-up needs and learn how to properly budget for projects. In addition, I talk about the importance of selecting a business name, logo, and corporate identity package that will promote your company's brand. You will find that building an online business is similar to launching a physical tutoring company.

Chapter 2: Selecting an Online Tutoring Platform

Just because you are providing online tutoring, it does not mean that all online tutoring platforms are created equal. As a result, you need good information to determine which platform works best for your online tutoring business. I provide guidelines to help you select a platform that will enable your clients to get the best results in the virtual classroom.

Chapter 3: Organizational Needs for Your Online Tutoring Business

In Chapter 3, you will learn about how you can find online clients and how to work with new and returning clients. I provide step-by-step details on how to implement my 13-step process for working with both new and returning clients. After reading this chapter, you will definitely be equipped to provide both data-driven instruction and quality customer service to your clients.

Chapter 4: Conducting Online Tutoring Sessions and Writing Monitoring Notes

By supplying data-driven instruction, you are required to provide quality online tutoring sessions and document the learner's progress. In Chapter 4, I discuss how to have a quality online tutoring session and write monitoring notes that will better represent the whole child in order to help him or her in the virtual classroom setting.

Where to Go From Here

You have the blueprint to get started, and you should be on the lookout for the next book in the *Expanding Your Tutoring Business Book Series*.

You can join our group at www.myonlinetutoringbusiness.com to to gain access to exclusive content and interact with Dr. Holland-Johnson so that you can strategically move your tutoring business from good to great.

Last but not least, if you are interested in networking with like-minded tutor business owners, join our FREE LinkedIn Group—My Online Tutoring Business.

Our LinkedIn Group is growing fast and group members are eager to connect with you and share their tutoring experiences with you. We truly have what you would call a Professional Learning Community.

You can also find more of her work at www.drholland-johnson. com. If you are interested in working with Dr. Holland-Johnson, please contact her using the contact form at her website.

Introduction

This book is very much needed in the tutoring industry as many learners are opting to receive instruction online or in the virtual classroom setting. In response to this demand, tutors need to have a blueprint that will help them build a quality online tutoring program.

This book has been created for the independent tutor or learning organization who desire to work with students online. My seminal work on tutoring, *Becoming a Better Tutor: A Data-Driven Approach to Tutoring,* has been well received since its first publication in 2010. In addition to my seminal work, I have authored the Expanding Your Tutoring Business Series that have also made a positive contribution to the tutoring industry.

This is my first comprehensive book regarding online tutoring; that is, it serves as the blueprint for individuals to start and operate their own quality online tutoring business. I'm a certified teacher, professional tutor, instructional designer, curriculum developer, online professor, educational consultant, and global business owner. I've stepped out on faith to follow my lifelong passion and dream. The information presented in this series is based on insight and actual experiences that I have encountered over the years in building my own global learning organization. I want to share with the world that online tutoring can be effective, but it takes a lot of planning, dedication, and know-how to avoid major pitfalls that come along with implementing a new program.

In this book, you'll find advice on how to position your learning organization to be in demand for online tutoring. My ultimate goal within my professional career and with this book is to inspire and transform others according to their life purpose.

Acknowledgments

I cannot say this enough, but I must give glory to God for helping me realize my potential and purpose in life. Thanks to my editor, Jena Roach, who has helped build confidence in my writing skills and challenged me to expand my ideas.

My Assumptions

In order to provide you with material to meet your unique situation, I had to make some basic assumptions about your tutoring business. I assume the following:

1. You already have started your tutoring practice and want to expand by offering online tutoring services.

2. You have a desire to tutor online and need this information to be successful in operating your online tutoring business.

3. You have working knowledge about tutoring.

4. You have read the other books in the Dr. Alicia Holland-Johnson's Expanding Your Tutoring Business Series.

Part I:
The Early Stages of Planning Your Online Tutoring Business

CHAPTER 1

Starting Up and Legalizing Your Tutoring Business

In this chapter:

- Creating a vision and mission statement
- Selecting a business name
- Filing for a business structure
- Selecting a logo and corporate identity package
- Assessing start-up needs and budgets

U p to this point, you have probably been doing business under an assumed name, which is fine. Are you ready to take your tutoring business to the next level? Before you can file for a business, you must create a vision and mission statement to help with selecting a business name and other identity for your tutoring business.

Creating a Vision and Mission Statement

You probably already have both a vision and mission statement in mind. If you are already running a home-based tutoring business, then you want to examine these statements to gain inspiration so that you can move your tutoring business forward.

Take a look at three powerful questions to help you create your vision and mission statement.

1. How many target market(s) do you plan to serve? Identify them.

_____

_____

_____

_____

_____

2. What is the purpose of your learning organization?

_____

_____

_____

_____

_____

3. How do you plan to serve your clients?

_____

_____

_____

_____

_____

> **Expert's Advice:** You may already know these answers, or you may need to see the logo before putting your vision on paper. Thus, I think that you should do what fits naturally.

Selecting a Business Name

Your business name will be how people recognize your services and products. In the business world, this is referred to as branding. You want to make your business stand out so others will know that you are unique. As a sole proprietor, you can be extremely creative or simple.

Select a business name that embodies both your vision and mission statement. Make it unique. In other words, choose wisely.

Please write down your answers to the following questions. Your responses will guide you in making the right choice about selecting a business name for your learning organization.

1. What does your business stand for?

_____

_____

_____

_____

2. When potential clients look at your business name, what would you like for them to see? Name at least seven adjectives.

_____

_____

_____

_____

Adjective List:

_____

_____

_____

_____

3. How would your business name define all the services and products?

_____

_____

_____

_____

4. Will your business name survive growth? Why or why not? Will the name of your company transition with future growth?

_____

_____

_____

_____

_____

5. List at least three potential business names, along with tag-lines, to represent the services and products offered.

_____

_____

_____

_____

_____

6. Ask trusted individuals which business name sounds professional. How did they respond?

_____

_____

_____

_____

7. What is your intuition telling you about your potential business name?

_____

_____

_____

_____

_____

Expert's Advice: Selecting the business name is the most important aspect of building a global learning organization. I know firsthand how selecting the right business name impacts the direction your organization will take.

When I started out locally as a private tutor, I was doing business as Realistic Measures & Consulting. At that time, my private home-based tutoring business was focusing on realistic results according to the student's learning needs. Thus, my tagline was "Believe in Yourself and Go Far"™.

After expanding my tutoring business into a learning organization, the business structure changed. It was the perfect time to reevaluate a new business name. In March 2011, iGlobal Educational Services was born.

iGlobal Educational Services was selected because our vision is to serve a global market, for which we are currently providing. While I still have the personal belief of "Believe in Yourself and Go Far," I kept my organization's new motto under this theme. iGlobal Educational Services' tagline is the following: "Believe. Inspire. Transform."™ It represents the past, present, and future of how my tutoring business has evolved into a great learning organization to help others.

Filing for a Business Structure

There are many business structures available to consider. You must visit your accountant or seek a free consultation to fully understand the options. Most tutoring companies are formed as Limited Liability Companies (LLC). However, there are other choices to choose from, which are outlined on the next page.

Sole Proprietary	Limited Liability Company	Partnership
• Working as an independent contractor.	• Owned by one or more individuals. • Members can function as a corporation. • Working as a company and hiring employees and/or independent contractors.	• Owned by two individuals. • Working as a company and hiring employees and/or independent contractors.

Scenario: "Merry-Go Round"

Destiny Purpose, a well-sought reading tutor in her community, anticipated an additional annual income of $5,000 just from her part-time tutoring. She operated her tutoring business as a sole proprietor and took on the assumed name of "Destiny's Tutoring Services." At the end of the tax year, she tallied all expenses related to her home-based business and quickly realized that she had spent over $1,000 and earned $5,000 in additional income.

For the past two years, she had been doing her own taxes using the online tax software. When she entered the required information, she was shocked to learn that she had to pay money to the Internal Revenue Service (IRS). That very next day, she called a local accountant and scheduled a free consultation. The accountant explained that those numbers were very likely because of her business structure, which was a sole proprietorship. Thus, the accountant recommended that she formed an LLC due to her specific tax information.

This business structure change would open up the door for promptly deducting business expenses and other perks. However, more paperwork is involved such as accounting, payroll and taxes, annual meetings with published minutes, and other required documentation. The accountant did say that a new business name would have to be established. Destiny was devastated because she knew how hard it would be to start over. However, she kept a positive attitude and thanked the accountant.

Expert's Advice: *Knowledge is power. It was wise of Destiny to contact this accountant because she was able to learn that she now needed to legalize her business as a corporation, a sub-chapter corporation for LLCs.*

From a business perspective, this is incredibly significant. Destiny started out as a sole proprietor to build her clientele and demand for her tutoring services. When it came time to take her business to the next level, she was able to do so. Since this is very new to her, I would recommend that Destiny continue to take steps to educate herself. This will help her build a dynamic learning organization.

Where to Look for Help

After deciding on a business structure and submitting the necessary legal paperwork, it is time to get some additional business insight. Did you know that there are organizations that are willing to help entrepreneurs, like yourself, start a new business?

Here are some places to help you get started:

1. SCORE
2. The Small Business Administration (SBA)
3. Publications [i.e. www.entrepreneur.com and www.becomingabettertutor.com]
4. Local University Small Business Development Center
5. City and State Resources

Selecting a Logo and Corporate Identity Package

This is one of the fun parts of starting a business! You will need to select a logo to set yourself apart from your competition. It is best to get a corporate identity package that includes a logo design, business card, and other design of your choice. However, if you are on a budget, try to get the logo first.

A typical corporate identity package will include the following items:

Typical Corporate Identity Package	
Item	**Purpose**
Logo Design	Sets your business apart from others. It's your brand name for your services and products.
Letterhead	Identifies communication from the company; this can be created by using only the logo files.
Business Card	Informs potential clients that you're in business. This is an absolute necessity for your tutoring company.
Post Card	Drives traffic to your tutoring business.
Presentation Folder	Shows professionalism with tutoring services.
Brochure Design	Showcases all services and products to potential clients.
Flyer	Drives traffic to your tutoring business.

Each of these marketing materials is very important. However, a priority list can be created based upon your tutoring business's needs.

Expert's Advice: From my own personal experience, I started out with the basic corporate identity package. This included a logo and business-card design. Typically logo designs can be saved in various formats, which results in saving money for a letterhead design.

Another necessity was a website. When I asked clients how they found me, the number one response was always online. Therefore, I made more investments in my website design and utilize other marketing strategies.

Assessing Start-Up Needs and Budget

If you are already in business, then this may be a breeze for you because you got everything that you already need, or so you think.

When starting a corporation, individuals will quickly learn that there are requirements that must be in place before getting an office space in a commercial setting or even taking on state and federal contracts.

Below is a list of items that you will need to budget:

1. Office Supplies
2. Office Space
3. Software
4. Marketing Materials
5. Payroll and Taxes
6. Office Technology
7. Business Insurances
8. Software
9. Outsourcing
10. Travel
11. Professional Development

Let's take a look at the various types of items that will need to be budgeted and why they are important to helping your tutoring business flourish.

Office Supplies Budget

The first item that will need to be budgeted is office supplies. This includes technology, software, and furniture.

Common office supplies that will be used regularly are listed below:

- Presentation folders
- File folders
- Label Maker
- Pens and Pencils

- Clipboard
- Boxes
- Jump drives
- CDs (recordable)
- Highlighters
- White-out
- Permanent markers
- Paper clips
- Color paper
- Envelopes (all sizes)
- Binder clips
- All-purpose copy paper
- Stapler (Heavy duty)

Office Technology

Common office technologies that will be used regularly are listed below:

- Fax machine
- Copier (Laser)
- iPad
- Lots of Ink and Toner
- Computers (Desktop and Laptop)
- Microphone Headset
- Phone Line
- Printer

Software

Common software for the office that will be used regularly is listed below:

- Microsoft Professional Office
- Adobe Creative Suite

- LiveScribe Pen
- My Attorney Software

Office Furniture

Common furniture for the office that will be used regularly is listed below:

- Bookcases
- Chairs and tables
- Conference table
- Receptionist desk
- Office desks
- Trash cans
- Filing cabinets (Secured)

In addition to these, you need to budget for miscellaneous items such as décor. While this budget does not have to be huge, careful consideration should be used when trying to decorate your office to create a positive business environment.

Even if your business is online, you still need to have your office decorated whether it is seasonal or year-round. This puts you in a professional frame of mind to complete your best work. Not to mention, if you do have clients who occasionally meet with you face-to-face, they will see that you are no amateur and conduct business as a professional.

Office Space Budget

The next item that you should budget for is office space. (See Dr. Holland-Johnson's *Expanding Your Tutoring Business: The Blueprint to Building a Global Learning Organization* for information on assessing your office space needs).

Whether you desire to work from home or at an alternative location, you will still need a place to do your work free of distractions and wandering eyes. When you are working with intellectual property you must protect it, even at your home.

Expert's Advice:

You may not think about it if you are working out of your home, but you need to save money now. As a sole proprietor, it may be so tempting to take and spend every dollar...and in some cases, you have to cover certain expenses. Thus, the goal is to save 25 percent of each project toward rent.

For instance, let's say that you made $1,000 per month for tutoring services.

From that, 10 percent of $1,000 is $100 while 5 percent of $1,000 is $50. Thus, when that amount is added, we have 25 percent of $1,000 is $250.

Based upon this example, this tutor should be saving $250 if he or she makes $1,000. In other words, individuals should be saving 25 percent of each project toward rent expenses that are occurred monthly.

I highly recommend reading and completing the exercises in Chapter 2 (See Dr. Holland-Johnson's *Expanding Your Tutoring Business: The Blueprint to Building a Global Learning Organization*) for information on assessing your office space needs and setting an office space budget. This will provide better insight into your tutoring business's needs and will help you plan appropriately.

Marketing Budget

The third item that you need to budget is marketing materials. While you may have a huge list ready to try to promote your tutoring business, it is best to choose your marketing strategies wisely. In my first tutoring book, *Becoming a Better Tutor: A Data-Driven Approach to Tutoring*, I mention that there are two types of marketing strategies. These include both basic and advanced marketing strategies.

Below is a table of each type of strategies listed under the appropriate marketing category:

Basic Marketing Strategies	Advanced Marketing Strategies
Online Advertising Local Advertising Networking	Offering Sponsorships Website Direct mailing and Newsletters Joining your Local Chamber of Commerce

(Holland-Johnson, 2010, pp. 28-29)

In addition to these listed strategies, individuals should be using more advanced strategies to connect with new and existing clients.

Don't assume that because your business is expanding, you also have to expand your marketing budget. This is not the case, though extra funds are beneficial when applying to those advanced marketing strategies such as press releases.

Payroll and Taxes Budget

The fourth item you will need to budget for is payroll and taxes. It is expected that employers set up an account with the state workforce agency. If you have hired a payroll company to help you with these needs, they will help manage this account when payroll is run each month. The main advantage of working with a payroll company is that they are held responsible. In fact, if there is an error on their behalf, they will pay for it.

Common tax reporting includes the following:

1. Sales and Use Tax

2. Franchise Tax

These types of taxes can be filed by you. When it comes time to start paying yourself, then you will need to start looking for experienced and trustworthy payroll companies that are cost-effective and exceptional in customer service. When hiring a company to do payroll and taxes, you should look for businesses that can provide full-service payroll and tax filings. It would not hurt to see if it also offers additional human resource services.

Expert's Advice:

You may think that it is not important to do payroll and taxes. This is only true if you are working as a sole proprietor because you get to keep what you make.

As a learning organization, it is very important to begin running payroll and reporting taxes. There are many organizations, including software that can calculate payroll and taxes. Depending on the state in which you are conducting business, there are certain requirements such as sales-tax and franchise-tax reporting.

When it comes to taxes at either the state or federal levels, it is best that you contact these tax agencies on your own. For example, Texas business owners would contact the state comptroller's office regarding any questions related to sales and tax use. When it comes to federal taxes, the best point of contact is the Internal Revenue Service (IRS).

Whether you decide to sell products or not, you are still required to apply for sales permit that lists your place of business.

When I expanded my tutoring business, all these taxes were very new to me. I quickly learned that I had made the best decision to start out as a home-based tutoring business. I searched online for local business courses for small business owners and was very blessed to find a workshop related to taxes. I was proud to pay $35 to attend this workshop because it helped me start out on the right road with business tax obligations.

Business Insurance Budget

The fifth item is to seek business insurance. If you get your own lease agreement, you will need business insurance prior to moving into the office space. Depending on your organizational structure, you will need (at minimum) the following types of business insurances.

1. Professional Liability

This type of insurance protects professional advice and service companies from negligence claims. For example, if you find yourself in a situation that may involve damages or other issues, then this will cover you and your business.

2. Automobile Insurance

If your business has vehicles that are used by tutors or to transport students, it is required to have this type of insurance. If your business does not have any vehicles for business use, then it is in your best interest to provide a written explanation when submitting bids to complete various projects. This is only if the project requires showing proof of business insurances and coverage.

3. Worker's Compensation Liability Insurance

This is another type of insurance that is needed to be in business. It covers any accidents on the job. Most state and federal contracts require worker's compensation liability insurance.

Outsourcing Budget

The sixth item that needs to be budgeted is outsourcing projects. There will be some projects that you will not have time to do or know how to do. Therefore, it is very important to pay an expert to complete them. For example, these projects can range from accounting writing, lead generation, and so forth.

> **Expert's Advice:** Don't enter into outsourcing thinking that you *do* not have to check on the contractor. In reality, you will have to lead them in order to get the desired outcome. Otherwise, you will become bitter and disappointed. You must understand what you want and provide written instructions.

Travel Budget

The seventh item is a travel budget. You will need to budget for travel, even if you work online. It is expected that you will attend professional development opportunities such as conferences or other informative opportunities. You may also need to budget for business trips that may be outside of your geographical area. Items that should be budgeted are the following:

Gas

Hotel

Meals

Toll fees

Air fare and associated fees

Bus fare

Taxi fare

Rentals

Professional Development Budget

The last item is professional development. Let's face it; no one knows everything. That's why we take courses to further our knowledge base. Specifically, in your tutoring business, there will be many things that you will need to learn to stay competitive in such a global economy.

Below are some recommended business courses to help you be successful with your tutoring business:

1. QuickBooks
2. Intellectual Property
3. Tax Requirement
4. Record-Keeping
5. Leadership
6. Customer Service
7. Social Media Marketing

While many conferences are offered throughout the year, it is very important to carefully select which ones you will attend. Traveling to conferences can be costly, but you get to see some very exciting places and meet different people from many walks of life.

You have been presented with good information that can help you begin to think about how you want to birth your learning organization. Proper planning and assessment of your tutoring business needs will lead you to a greater chance of success with your organization.

CHAPTER 2
Selecting an Online Tutoring Platform

You may be ready to start your e-learning or online tutoring program, but there are several tasks that must be considered. These tasks include the following: (a) Finding a suitable online tutoring platform; (b) Creating a process that will make your online tutoring business run smoothly; (c) Creating a plan for conducting online tutoring sessions and data-reporting; and (d) Addressing how to communicate within the virtual classroom. Each of these tasks will be discussed along the way as you read each chapter in this book.

Guidelines for Selecting an Online Tutoring Platform

When it comes time to selecting an online tutoring platform, you need to be aware of the many platforms available. In addition, you need to make sure that you are catering to your clients' needs, not just your budget. With this perspective, you can be better prepared before you make your selection. To help with this process, there are some questions that will guide you into making a well-informed decision. Let's look at these questions on the next page.

1. How will you record attendance to verify that learners came to sessions?

_____

_____

_____

_____

_____

2. Will the virtual classroom accommodate all learning modalities? Why or why not?

_____

_____

_____

_____

_____

3. What is the pricing for the virtual platform? Does it include annual licensing fees?

_____

_____

_____

_____

_____

4. Will the virtual classroom accommodate all learning modalities? Why or why not?

_____

_____

_____

_____

_____

5. What is the pricing for the virtual platform? Does it include annual licensing fees?

_____

_____

_____

_____

_____

6. How will clients log-on to the system? Is there a sign-in page or will you send them session links?

_____

_____

_____

_____

_____

7. What are your administrative tasks, and how will they impact you conducting online tutoring sessions?

_____

_____

_____

_____

_____

Expert's Advice: These are some questions to get you thinking about your online tutoring program. I want to share with you my top capabilities in a virtual classroom. This will be very important if you plan on working with other organizations to provide online tutoring services. You have to understand that online tutoring is still relatively new. As a result, you must be able to deliver so that your business will soar and your efforts will help promote online tutoring in a positive fashion.

Expert's Advice: *(continued)*

Here's what your online tutoring business should have for its e-learning program and my rationale behind it:

1. *Chat Feature*

a. *Benefit for Students:* The chat feature is used primarily for interacting with class, if more learners are present. If not, then this is an individual way of asking questions for the tutor.

b. *Benefit for Tutors:* Tutors are able to pose questions, write directions, or view problems in the chat feature. This comes in handy so that students can actually see the problem. Also, you need to check to see if there is a copy-and-paste feature so that it saves them.

c. *Learning Styles Addressed:* kinesthetic, tactile, and visual.

2. *Whiteboard (With Multiple Boards)*

a. *Benefit for Students:* The learners are able to use their visual learning style. They are able to write on the whiteboard, which makes it an interactive lesson. For example, if students need to explain their thinking, then they can draw it on the whiteboard.

b. *Benefit for Tutors:* Tutors are able to reference more than one whiteboard at a time. Tutors have the ability to restrict learner access on the whiteboard, if deemed necessary. Tutors are able to deliver instruction, just as they were in a traditional classroom that either had a whiteboard or interactive whiteboard.

c. *Learning Styles Addressed:* kinesthetic, tactile, and visual.

3. *Webcam*

a. *Benefits:* There should be a webcam feature available so that you can see the learner and he or she can see you. This will take the guesswork out of whether you are tutoring that learner or not. You can actually see him or her and he or she can see you.

Please note that you will only be able to see their face and surrounding area where the camera is displayed. Depending on whether you are using a laptop or desktop, it will determine if your clients are able to see you. This will be an added benefit to your online tutoring program. It will definitely add credibility that real tutors are being used in online tutoring sessions.

b. *Learning Styles Addressed:* visual

4. *Media*

a. *Benefits:* A virtual classroom should have the capability of playing media in the classroom. Often times, tutors will enhance their lessons by providing two- to three-minute (no more than five minutes) video clips to show how the concepts are tied to the real world and so forth. In addition to the chat and interactive whiteboard feature, this feature makes the learning environment more conducive to engaging and interesting tutoring sessions.

b. *Learning Styles Addressed:* visual

5. *Recording Feature*

a. *Benefits:* You want to make sure that all interaction in the classroom can be recorded for multiple purposes.

The first purpose is to provide documentation that actual tutoring sessions are being conducted and authorized individuals can view the session recordings to verify this information.

The second purpose is to improve the quality of tutoring sessions, while the third purpose is to evaluate tutor performance and allow tutors to self-evaluate their tutoring sessions.

b. *Learning Styles Addressed:* visual

Expert's Advice: *(continued)*

6. *Capability to View and Send a Variety of Files*

a. *Benefit for Students:* Just like the traditional setting, both tutors and learners will be expected to view and send a variety of files. For example, students may need assistance with a certain set of problems, which will have to be uploaded to the tutor.

b. *Benefit for Tutors:* Tutors want to also be able to view documents on the whiteboard so that learners are able to view a presentation or work a few problems together.

c. *Learning Styles Addressed:* kinesthetic, tactile, and visual.

7. *Automated Attendance Report*

a. *Benefits:* You need to make sure the virtual classroom has an attendance feature that captures both the tutor and participant time spent in the classroom. It also needs to capture the overall time spent in the tutoring session and the names of all participants involved in the tutoring session.

When you are shopping for a virtual classroom platform, these are the requirements that should be critical to your e-learning program. Most importantly, it will help you have the foundation necessary to deliver top-notch instruction to your clients.

b. *Learning Styles Addressed:* visual

8. *Group Participant Features*

a. *Benefits:* You may not be offering group-tutoring sessions at the moment, but you should purchase a virtual classroom platform that has the capability to plan for future organizational needs. There are virtual classrooms that can hold up to at least 10 or more participants at one time.

Expert's Advice: *(continued)*

This feature can also be used to host your organizational trainings and monthly meetings. This depends on how your tutoring business is structured and how your business is run. In my professional opinion, you want to save as much money as possible where you can without jeopardizing payroll or other important organizational needs. If you research online, you will discover that the costs are very expensive and may not make sense if you are a small tutoring company. Therefore, it would be in your best interest to select an online tutoring platform that can also be used for training purposes.

b. *Learning Styles Addressed:* kinesthetic, tactile, and visual.

9. *Sign-In/Log-In Features*

a. *Benefits:* Ideally, this is where you want to have your clients log-in from your own website. Depending on your finances, you may want to make an initial investment by starting small rather than shelling out a lot of loot that will be used for other purposes to run your tutoring business.

There are virtual classrooms that have session links that can be emailed to tutors and clients. Just a heads up, this is a lot of work, but you can learn a lot about how your virtual classroom interface works. This will strictly depend on your budget for this aspect of your tutoring business.

b. *Learning Styles Addressed:* kinesthetic, tactile, and visual.

Scenario: "Let's Have a Chat Only Class"

Desmond, a Supplemental Educational Services (SES) Provider, decides that he will apply to become a SES provider in another state, besides the one in which he resides. His proposed tutoring program only has the chat feature and a whiteboard. His tutors do not speak English, but they are very knowledgeable in the subject area and are highly educated. His organization has been successful globally and has a track record of helping students that cater to visual learning.

1. How could Desmond improve his tutoring program for *all* students?

_____

_____

_____

_____

_____

2. From an organizational standpoint, what type of training is required for chat-only tutors? Are there training scripts for tutors in their home language? How is this handled?

_____

_____

_____

_____

_____

3. From a parental perspective, would you want your child to receive tutoring from this provider? Why or why not? How does your child like to learn?

_____

_____

_____

* *

Scenario: "A Heaven-Sent Deal...Really?"

Jaimaica Johnson serves her community by offering both math and reading tutoring. She was recently offered a state contract under the federal No Child Left Behind (NCLB) Act and really had to look for an online tutoring platform. Not to mention, she did not have any tutors on board so she panicked.

One beautiful day, she checked her email and found an email from a company who offered both an online tutoring platform and their tutors. Can you imagine how Jaimaica felt? Initially, she was very excited about the offer until she found out the details and saw the contract. In a nutshell, Jaimaica figured that she would pay an annual license fee for $1,000 plus a monthly fee based upon the number of students served. Not to mention, the contract stated that she had to pay the monthly fee whether students were present or not. Last but not least, she was still responsible for paying the tutors, but could not train or communicate with them. After several days of thinking about this deal and realizing in the contract that these tutors could not offer Reading/ English Language Arts (ELA) tutoring, Jaimaica quickly turned down the offer and opted to do it herself.

* *

1. Do you think that Jaimaica made the right decision? Why or why not?

_____

_____

_____

_____

_____

2. From an organizational standpoint, what type of business sense did this make, if any?

_____

_____

_____

_____

_____

3. What are your recommendations to Jaimaica?

_____

_____

_____

_____

_____

Scenario: "Designing on a Quarter"

Justin Davis had searched around, but had not found the virtual classroom platform that met his organizational needs and was cost-effective for an emerging tutor business. Disgusted with his options, Justin decided that he would fund the design of his own virtual classroom. When he started talking to developers, he was quoted at least $15K to build requirements that met 95 percent of his organizational needs. Justin had to make the decision to continue face-to-face tutoring sessions until he could afford the online tutoring platform.

1. Do you think that Justin should give up or wait? Why or why not?

_____

_____

_____

_____

_____

2. How could have Justin benefitted from finding a cost-effective online tutoring program?

_____

_____

_____

_____

3. Do you think that it is worthwhile to create a proprietary online tutoring platform in a market that is saturated? Why or why not?

_____

_____

_____

_____

_____

CHAPTER 3
Organizational Needs for Your Online Tutoring Business

When you are operating an online tutoring business, it takes a lot of preparation. It is totally different than running an on-ground learning organization. In this chapter, I take you through finding clients, managing and working clients, and how to be successful with your tutoring business from an organizational perspective.

Finding New Clients

Let's look at how to bring clients to your tutoring business. It's important to start thinking about the following questions:

1. How will I market my tutoring business?

2. Will I need a website or how can I improve my current website?

3. Who are my potential clients?

Have you answered these questions? If not, it's okay, because we will take a look at the many ways to advertise your tutoring business. If you have answered all these questions and are already tutoring, then maybe it's time to look at other avenues of attracting customers to your business. Let's look at two categories of marketing your services in the tutoring industry—basic marketing strategies and advanced marketing strategies.

Basic Marketing Strategies

Basic marketing strategies are strategies that have low costs and are easy to use when first starting your tutoring business. Oftentimes you are using these strategies and may not even know it. We will explore a few of the marketing strategies that can be used to attract clients to you. These strategies are the following: (1) online advertising, (2) local advertising, and (3) networking.

Online Advertising

Many jobs are being posted online, especially on job search websites, such as Yahoo Jobs. In today's society, there are many tutoring sites where you can post your tutoring profile for a nominal fee. I have used social networking sites, such as Facebook, Twitter, and LinkedIn, as avenues for advertising my services. I also use Craigslist to advertise my services, as Craigslist allows one to post services in numerous categories. In other words, there will only be one copy of the posting visible. Otherwise, Craigslist monitors postings, and if they see that there is a similar or repeated posting, then they will delete the message or flag it as spam. Please use your own judgment when posting and applying for tutoring jobs, as there seem to be scams targeted at tutors. A good rule of thumb is to post only in your area "that›s if you conduct your tutoring sessions in your own home or at your client›s home" and respond to potential clients who are within your geographic region.

Local Advertising

If you prefer to post locally, then you should seek locations where there's a great deal of traffic. While posting flyers in schools may be a great idea, many public school districts do not allow advertisements about tutoring. Others have a rigid, tedious process where one may have to wait several months before gaining exposure. For this reason, I recommend posting services in areas where you are allowed. You could even consider offering your current client an incentive to refer others to your tutoring services.

After clients have made a decision to choose my tutoring services, I offer them a referral coupon so that they can refer others to my tutoring business. In exchange, clients are able to get a free or discounted tutoring session. Word of mouth is the best way to advertise, since potential clients are already aware of how you conduct business as a tutor and have testimonies about their child›s successes. If you show gratification to your satisfied clients, your business will continue to grow.

Networking

Networking is important in every industry. If you are tutoring locally, then it would make sense to partner or serve as a vendor at a local event to market your services. Oftentimes other small businesses will allow you to advertise in their buildings in exchange for the same exposure and/or services. For example, there was a small business owner who owned a salon and whose daughter needed assistance in math, and we informally discussed tutoring in general while I got my hair done. The following day, we held a tutoring consultation and entered into an agreement that for each six sessions she would give me one free hairstyle. This hairstyle ranged from $180.00 upward. After the tutoring consultation, I realized that her daughter only needed six sessions to improve her area of weakness. In this case, both parties were happy. The stylist was able to get the help for her daughter, and I was happy to help her daughter. From a business perspective, each owner demonstrated honesty and commitment and was results-oriented, which resulted in numerous referrals.

Please beware that every client will not be willing to enter such an agreement and tutors should be selective. In any event, networking is a strategy that should be considered, especially if you are a small business owner.

Advanced Marketing Strategies

Advanced marketing strategies are strategies that are used when a business is established and is lucrative enought to attract more clients. We will explore a few of the marketing strategies that can be used to expand your marketing repertoire.

These strategies are the following: (1) offering sponsorships, (2) getting a website started, (3) using direct mailing and newsletters, and (4) joining your local Chamber of Commerce.

Offering Sponsorships

Are you into sports? Local youth sport coaches are always looking for business owners or individuals to sponsor them. This includes providing certain things for them, like buying their uniforms and equipment. This type of sponsorship will allow you visibility with your targeted audience if you plan on working with K-12 students.

Another way to advertise your tutoring business is to sponsor other community events, such as a luncheon for an event. Let's say that you belong to a professional organization; you can always sponsor a lunch or set up a booth that displays your tutoring services. You never know who's from your geographical area.

Getting a Website Started

A website will be a good investment because clients are always surfing the Internet and could easily find your services. There are many web-hosting services available to choose from, such as godaddy. com, yahoo.com, google.com, and others.

When creating your website, please include the following: (1) a home page with an advertisement about your services, (2) services that you offer, (3) information about the company, and (4) contact page for potential clients.

Home Page

Your home page should consist of your advertisement and should entice prospective clients to want to know more about your services. It wouldn't hurt to add a picture or a logo that brands your tutoring business. This is the first place that potential clients will stop, and it should accurately reflect your tutoring business.

Services Page

This is where you should explain why clients should choose you as a private tutor. After that you should list the services that you provide, along with any pricing information. For example, my potential clients must e-mail or call for current rates. This allows you to interact directly with them, enabling you to justify your rates. You may also want to include a column titled, "What's New at [Your Tutoring Business]." In this section you should include any events that have recently occurred or any upcoming events.

About [Your Tutoring Business]'s Page

This is where you provide the history of your tutoring business and how it got started. Most people are interested in how this service becomes available to others. This would also be a great place to post client testimonials to confirm that you do offer high-quality services to your clients.

Contact Us

On your contact page, it's important to have the phone number, address, and e-mail address of your business. Also, if your web servicer has the capability, it would be helpful to have a link for clients to find driving directions to your tutoring business.

In addition, it would be a great idea to include a customer contact form, which allows potential clients to ask questions about your tutoring services and leave their contact information. This allows you to contact them and answer any questions that they may have about your tutoring services.

Using Direct Mailing and Promotional Products

Direct mailing is a marketing strategy worth trying once your business has grown. You can either choose to mail out your marketing materials or use online direct marketing services. In either case, you would need to create a contact list or purchase a contact list of potential clients who may be interested in your tutoring services.

There are various companies you can use to purchase contact information, such as geoselector.com. Promotional products are definitely a great way to give your tutoring business a jump start. These items could be small, such as mouse pads, pens, pencils, notepads, key chains, and other inexpensive items. Ideally, these items would be given out to first-time clients or prospective clients.

Joining Your Local Chamber of Commerce

Does the area where you are locating your tutoring business have a Chamber of Commerce? If so, you should strongly consider joining it once you have found an office space. The investment that you make with the Chamber of Commerce will definitely go a long way for your business. This organization is dedicated to helping new businesses flourish and will provide a network of resources to help build your tutoring business.

It really does not matter which marketing method you use; you should use the strategies that yield the most traffic yet are cost-efficient to your tutoring business. The bottom line is that you stay within your marketing budget while letting your potential clients know that you offer a variety of services that are tailored to them.

Working with New and Returning Clients

You have been marketing for some time now and have found a couple of clients. Are you wondering what should come next for these clients? It's clear that tutoring should occur, but there really is more involved. There's actually a 13-step process that you need to follow. Don't worry…I won't present them all at once, but I will show you a diagram to at least give you an idea before diving into the details for each step.

13-Step Process for Working with New and Returning Clients

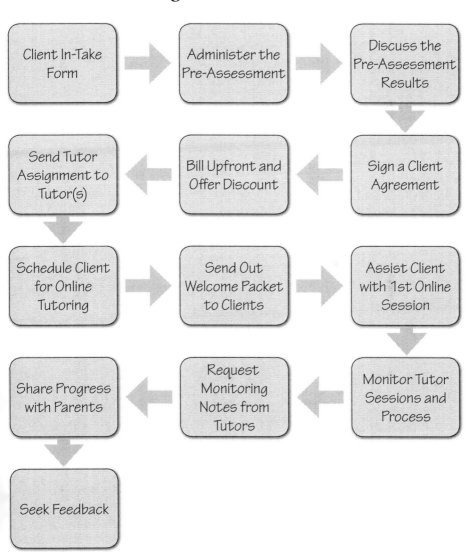

Step 1: Fill the Client In-Take Form

You may be eager to take on this client, but you really need to assess whether you can help him or her. You will do this by scheduling an online tutor consultation or phone consultation. More than likely, you have the basic information in which you need when he or she first inquired. If clients do not have access to the Internet, you may want to complete this information as well.

Here's what you need to know regarding the client intake form:

- Why does the learner need tutoring?
- What is the learner's academic situation?
- How does the learner prefer to learn?
- What is the learner's academic history?
- How does the learner view his or her education?

These are five questions that will definitely help you understand whether you are able to help the learner with his or her academic needs. If these questions are answered, then it will be time to move on to the next step in the 13-step process.

The most important thing is to make sure that the client has his or her own computer or access to one before beginning any tutoring services. Otherwise, he or she cannot benefit from your online tutoring services.

• •

Scenario: "FREE means FREE"

Destiny, a SES Tutor Provider, offers an online tutoring program for at-risk students for FREE under the NCLB Act. In her state application, she listed that students would need to have access from their own computers. However, scholarships were available for families who may need a computer for their child. Given that the Per Pupil Allocation (PPA) is on average $1,000, she thought that she would be able to recoup the cost after providing several hours of tutoring services. She never tells the clients that they will keep the computer, but it is very likely because they may not return it.

Destiny finally got her chance to provide a scholarship to a family in need. The intake process went smoothly and computers and mobile Internet devices were shipped to the student. Several days later, Destiny called to begin online tutoring services and was very surprised. The family did not answer her calls, but confirmed that they did receive the technology on a voicemail message left on her office phone. Destiny was very upset, but she chalked it up as experience and moved on. However, at the next board meeting, the policy of providing scholarship to families was amended where no technology would be offered to clients.

• •

1. Do you think that Destiny did the right thing in this situation? Why or why not?

_____

_____

_____

_____

2. From an organizational perspective, how would you have handled this situation?

_____

_____

_____

_____

3. From a parental perspective, how would you feel about a tutoring company who provided your child with both FREE tutoring and learning tools?

_____

_____

_____

_____

Expert's Advice: First of all, it is very unfortunate that the parents missed the opportunity to help their child with their learning needs. Secondly, it is such a shame that Destiny lost revenue due to an unfortunate situation. The reality is that Destiny is in business and must understand that she has to do what is best in the interest of her business. Let me be very clear—Destiny showed compassion and good faith of providing learning tools for the family. In this particular situation, she was looking out for the best interest of students. However, it was the parent who took the ball and ran with it, so to speak. In other words, the parents did their own child injustice, not Destiny.

These are situations in which the state should investigate because it is very unfair to SES providers, such as Destiny. If the client intake process goes smoothly, then it is time to proceed to Step 2, which is to administer the pre-assessments.

Step 2: Administer the Pre-Assessment

In Step 2, this is where you would need to administer the pre-assessment. Depending on how you run your learning organization, you may opt to have students come to the office or take their pre-assessment online. Whatever the method, a pre-assessment should be on file to assess the impact of the tutoring program.

If you are administering an online pre-assessment, you will need to provide directions to help them access the online pre-assessment. Below are sample directions to provide to your clients:

Directions for taking Your Online Pre-Assessment

1. Click on the following web link:
www.linkforonlinepreassessmentgoeshere.com

2. Locate Student Login and Click It.

3. Once you have Clicked On it, you will see a screen that has "Student Login."

4. Please type in your assigned login and password. This will help identify you as the person who is taking this assessment.

5. Your assigned username and password are listed below:

Username: HollandJohnson3
Password: 593test

6. Click "Login" to begin the test.

What Happens After I Complete My Test?

It will tell you that you are finished with your test.

How do these test results help me?

These test results help us build lessons for you and measure your progress throughout your online tutoring program. Thus, it is very important for you to take these tests seriously and do your personal best.

If you have any questions or technical support, please contact [insert contact name] at [Insert Phone Number]. You can also reach me directly at [insert phone number] or via email at [youremailaddress@gmail.com].

Good Luck on your test!
[Your Tutoring Business Name]

Step 3: Discuss the Pre-Assessment Results

After the pre-assessment has been taken, it is only natural to discuss the results with the parent. This is the opportunity to seek feedback from the parent and student. It is best to perform these interviews separately because the learner may not always open up while the parent is present.

Below are some sample questions to ask both parents and the learner:

Parent Questions:

1. Are there any other concepts that should be addressed that were not evident in the pre-assessment results? If so, what are they?

2. Do you have any further questions or concerns?

Learner Questions:

1. How do you think that you did on your pre-assessment?

2. Are there specific concepts we need to work on?

3. How do you want us to help you?

These are some questions that can help you with the intake process.

Expert's Advice: The good thing about online pre-assessments is that the results are immediate and depending on the software used for these assessments, detailed reports are available for both parents and tutor business owners.

Once pre-assessment results have been discussed, this is the appropriate time to schedule the client and seek deposits. If this is a client from a federal contract, then you will not need to do this. Once services begin, you can bill the school district.

If you are working with private clients, you should charge for pre-assessments.

Step 4: Sign a Client Agreement Regarding Sessions

At this point in the process, it is deemed necessary to have the client sign a client agreement before doing a lot of administrative work that goes along with new clients. Below are some questions to help you build your own client agreement regarding online tutoring sessions. They are the following:

1. What is your policy regarding assessments? Are clients responsible for payment? Why or why not?

_____

_____

_____

_____

_____

2. What are the tutoring fees?

_____

_____

_____

_____

3. What are the methods of payment? How do you feel about accepting checks?

_____

_____

_____

_____

4. How would you describe the recommended tutoring program?

_____

_____

_____

_____

5. What is the policy for attending online tutoring sessions?

_____

_____

_____

_____

_____

6. How are cancellations handled?

_____

_____

_____

_____

_____

7. What is the policy for "no shows" for both tutors and clients?

_____

_____

_____

_____

_____

8. What are the available tutoring times?

_____

_____

_____

_____

9. What is the policy regarding severe weather and emergencies?

_____

_____

_____

_____

_____

10. What is the scope of the agreement?

_____

_____

_____

_____

11. What is the policy regarding divulging personal information?

_____

_____

_____

_____

12. What is the policy for violating the client agreement?

_____

_____

_____

_____

13. How will clients return the form and sign it? Will it be electronically or via fax?

_____

_____

_____

_____

These are some questions to help you get started with building your very own client agreement.

These next few steps will be done all at once, but want to address each of them separately.

Step 5: Bill Upfront and Offer a Discount

By this time, clients are serious. You need to collect the funds or a non-refundable deposit. Often times, clients may not be able to provide the entire balance so you may want to offer a payment plan, such as 50 percent before the first session, and the other 50 percent before the third session. This method works best when offering tutoring packages. In any event, you should be using invoices with your clients, in programs such as QuickBooks.

> **Expert's Advice:** I highly recommend reading my other books and taking my online tutoring course: Tutor 104: Marketing Your Tutoring Business. These resources will provide you the support necessary with pricing strategies.

Step 6: Send Tutor Assignment to Tutor(s)

Rather than putting the cart before the horse, once Steps 4 and 5 have been completed, this is the appropriate time to seek a qualified tutor in the respective tutoring area. Below are some questions to think about when making tutoring assignments:

1. What is the tutor's availability?

_____

_____

_____

_____

_____

2. What is the tutor's subject area?

_____

_____

_____

_____

_____

3. What did the tutor's performance results?

_____

_____

_____

_____

_____

4. How will this tutor impact the client? Will it be a good fit? Why or why not?

_____

_____

_____

_____

_____

5. What is the tutor's assignment completion rate?

_____

_____

_____

_____

_____

These five questions will aid in placing the best tutors in tutoring assignments that will be a win/win for all. Let's look at a sample tutoring assignment that can be sent via email to a tutor.

Good Afternoon, [Insert Tutor's Name],

Happy Friday! We have an online math tutoring assignment available. It is the following:

9th Grade

Currently, we are waiting to hear back from the school district. It will take anywhere from 1-7 business days for the school district to approve the Student Learning Plan (SLP).

This student has 24 hours and 23 minutes of tutoring hours.

The parent has requested the following tutoring schedule:

Mondays   4:00-5:30PM CST
Tuesdays   4:00-5:30PM CST
Thursdays   4:00-5:30PM CST

Please reply back by Monday, June 18, 2012 (5pm CST) close of business indicating whether you accept or decline this tutoring assignment.

Looking forward to your response,
[Insert Your Name or Tutor Director's Name]

Step 7: Schedule Client for Online Tutoring

Let's be clear; this is about your client. However, it is very important to let clients know when tutors are available. In reality, there cannot be one without the other. In light of this, you need to have the tutor's availability handy as the client is providing his or her schedule. This will increase your chances of getting the client scheduled.

Let's look at two different scenarios to help you understand the importance of having a process in order.

• •

Scenario: "If they can, So can I"

Shelly, a science tutor, took on a tutoring assignment and both parties were content. About 2/3 of the tutoring program, the client missed two sessions and the tutor was paid according to the company's compensa-

tion policy. Without advanced warning, the tutor did not show up to the next scheduled tutoring session. Luckily, the tutor business owner also tutored in that subject area. Therefore, he took over the assignment. As for Shelley, she was coached and a "no show" was recorded in her performance record.

• •

1. How would you have handled this situation, if you were the tutor business owner?

_____

_____

_____

_____

_____

2. Do you think Shelley had that right? Why or why not?

_____

_____

_____

_____

• •

Scenario: "Tutoring or Work—Which One?"

Danielle, a working mom, signed her children up for tutoring when she realized that they had an opportunity to receive free tutoring. Initially, she was very excited about the opportunity and her two girls attended the sessions faithfully...until her mom got a new job.

Rather than let the tutoring company know, Danielle stopped her children from attending because the tutoring times did not work for her. She decided that a later time would have to work. The tutoring company was able to accommodate the family and the two girls finished their 9-week tutoring program.

• •

1. Do you think this was a reasonable accommodation? Why or why not?

_____

_____

_____

_____

_____

2. How would you have handled this situation?

_____

_____

_____

_____

3. How could this been avoided? Was it possible? Why or why not?

_____

_____

_____

_____

_____

Expert's Advice: In Scenario 2: "Tutoring or Work—Which One?", this could not be avoided. The best advice is to work with the parent because she is already under stress. If it turns out that the learner will have a great deal of time pass until the next tutoring session, then it is best to explain to the parent why you cannot work with their child again. The bottom line is that tutoring should not be viewed as an added burden to the client or tutor.

Step 8: Send Out Welcome Packets to Clients

Most of your clients may have their first tutoring experience with you. Therefore, you need to have a welcome packet for your clients (and new tutors, too). Specifically, our focus is on online tutoring businesses and we need to look at welcome packets according to this mode of instruction. Let's look at the components of a welcome packet for new online clients:

a. Welcome Letter from the President

b. Sales Copy and Business Card

c. Hours of Operation/Scheduled Holidays

d. What to Expect

e. Program Survey

f. White Paper—Condensed Form

g. Session and Recording Links or Login Information

h. Contact/Tech Support Information

i. Late Session Policy/Tutor Agreement

j. Tutoring Schedule/Instructional Plan

k. Complimentary e-book

l. Promotional product

m. Monthly Newsletters

n. Access to Your Blog

A. Welcome Letter

This sends a nice, warm welcome that can make another good impression for your company.

> **Expert's Advice:** You really have to understand that you are working with families and should be building a relationship rather than looking at each tutoring agreement. The reality is that you are running a business, but always remember that PEOPLE come first. If you approach your business in this manner, you will make a significant difference in the lives of your clients.

B. Sales Copy and Business Cards

This is the appropriate time to include your marketing material, which could be a brochure or one-sheet page regarding your tutoring services. In addition to this sales copy, you should also include a business card. It is best practice to include at least two business cards. This can be a great way to get your tutoring business noticed and out into the community. It is also a good idea to ask them to share your business card with a friend.

C. Hours of Operation/Scheduled Holidays

If you have not told your clients, then you will need to let them know about the hours of operation and any scheduled holidays.

Below are some typical hours of operation and scheduled holiday closings:

Hours of Operations

Monday thru Friday	12-8pm CST
Saturday	10-2pm CST
Sunday	4-8pm CST

Scheduled Holidays

Spring Break	Summer Break
Fall Break	Winter Break
President's Day	Valentine's Day
Martin Luther King Jr. Day	Memorial Day

These are some examples that can be used to help you plan your hours of operations and scheduled holidays.

D. What to Expect

This is your opportunity to explain to client what they can expect. Often times, when you speak with them again, they may not have the exact details. Therefore, this is just another added benefit for your clients. Here are some questions to help draft a one-page checklist of what can be expected:

1. What can clients expect regarding tutoring services?

2. How often will progress be reported?

3. What days and times are available for online tutoring services?

4. What are the tutor qualifications for the specific tutor assigned to clients?

5. How will you communicate to clients and what is the time-frame in which you will do so?

E. Program Survey

You may place a copy of the program survey or at least mention it to clients so that they are aware of customer feedback. You may also opt to later email it to clients who have provided an email address close to the end of their online tutoring program.

F. White Paper (Condensed)

This is an opportunity to educate your clients about the education industry, specifically regarding tutoring.

G. Session Links/Log-In Information

You will need to provide the log-in information and/or session links so that clients can log in to the virtual classroom successfully.

H. Contact/Tech Support Information

There will be technological glitches as is expected with technology. However, you should provide the contact information so that clients know how to reach the office.

I. Client Agreement

A copy of the client agreement should be included for easy access, along with company policy regarding tutoring services.

J. Tutoring Schedule with Student Learning Plan (SLP)

A copy of the SLP should be included so that clients will know what needs to be covered throughout the online tutoring program. In addition, it is very important to include the tutoring schedule.

K. Complimentary Book or e-book

Clients would appreciate a free resource to help their children at home. When you are providing resources, the focus should be on your clients, not trying to sell your company.

L. Promotional Products

It is a great idea to provide your client with a meaningful promo product that can get your tutoring business exposure, as well as, help them. This is another small token that will set your tutoring business apart.

M. Monthly Newsletters

A copy of the most recent monthly newsletters for clients should be included as well.

N. Information about your Company's Blog

Another great way to connect with clients is to provide a blog that can help them with their children. Visit www.parentseducatechildren.blogspot.com to see an example of how a blog might work for your tutoring business.

These are some components or items that should be included in your tutor company's Welcome Packet for new clients.

Step 9: Assist Client with First Online Tutoring Session

Just like any other new concept, support is needed. You may decide that you want to send out written instructions, but you will still need to follow-up with a phone call. This call should be made at least 30 minutes before the scheduled tutoring session.

Please know that you may need to help the client more than once to ensure that they are successful with logging into the course.

Step 10: Monitor Tutoring Sessions and Progress

Clients and tutors should be made aware that all online tutoring sessions are recorded and will be monitored. This is very important if documentation must be submitted to school districts or if you are seeing recording links to clients pertaining to only their child.

This step keeps your online tutoring sessions in quality shape with the recording feature of the virtual classroom. This is also an important step for monitoring tutor's progress when it comes to performance review time.

Step 11: Request Monitoring Notes from Tutors

In Step 11, it is very important to receive monitoring notes from tutors in a timely manner. It is recommended that you allow tutors at least 48 business hours to turn in those reports. You will need a process to manage these monitoring notes because you end up having 8-12 monitoring notes for each client.

Step 12: Share Progress With Parents

You should send out monitoring notes to clients within 72 business hours. In the event that the client attends two to three days a week, it may be more feasible to send out a brief weekly update and a detailed monthly progress report.

You may send them via mail or email. Before you do though, please ask the parents their preferred method of contact. When in doubt, send those reports via mail, preferably certified mail.

> **Expert's Advice:** I highly recommend using an online program such as Google docs or Dropbox to manage these files. Once you start getting a lot of clients, you will appreciate my advice and understand the importance and value of these notes. Monitoring notes should be used to create the monthly progress report for your clients. Let's face it...the tutor will know first-hand how a learner performs.

Step 13: Seek Feedback Regarding Your Online Tutoring Program

You will need feedback from parents, students, and tutors to truly gain insight into how to improve your online tutoring program. I strongly encourage you to use online survey programs such as survey monkey to help with managing, collecting, and analyzing data. This should be done at the very end of the learner's online tutoring program.

In this chapter, you had an opportunity to learn about the 13-step progress of working with both new and returning clients. Each of these steps will help increase your organizational practices and reputation as an effective online tutoring company.

CHAPTER 4
Conducting Online Tutoring Sessions and Writing Monitoring Notes

If you have been tutoring for some time in person, you have a general idea of how a tutoring session should open. In your quest of becoming an online tutor, you will experience many online tutoring platforms. No matter the platform, you still need to know how to conduct online tutoring sessions. In this chapter, I will share with you strategies to have a productive tutoring session.

Opening an Online Tutoring Session

The first step is to get online and get connected into the virtual classroom. Once this is done, it is time to get set up so that valuable tutoring session time is not wasted on organization. Here's a chart to help summary the steps that should be taken when setting up for an online tutoring session.

Importance of Early Arrival in the Virtual Classroom

If you are using a virtual classroom platform, you will need to enter the classroom at least 10-15 minutes before your client so that you can set up your lesson. Typically, tutors upload necessary files to the whiteboard and post a welcome message for the client.

Posting a Welcome Message in the Virtual Classroom

The welcome message should be warm and make the learner feel at ease when working online with you. The welcome message should also include the learning objective(s), tutoring session agenda, and a quick reminder to make sure that he or she types in either his or her first and last name.

Below is a sample welcome message:

Welcome to Our Online Tutoring Session, [Insert Learner's Name]!

Please take a moment and type both your first and last name.

Please solve the problem in the chat window. You can show your work on the whiteboard.

Today's Tutoring Session Agenda

   1 Problem Solving Strategies

   2 Solving Word Problems

   3 Mini-Assessment

   4 Closure

Look forward to working with you,
Your Favorite Online Tutor

This should be written at the beginning of every tutoring session prior to the learner entering the classroom. That way, the learner can spend time learning what he or she will be learning for that specific tutoring session and it will be using tutoring session time wisely.

Posting Warm-Up Questions in the Virtual Classroom

It's always a good idea to get your learner warmed-up with some sort of problem or writing prompt. It should not be a challenge, but it is a good way to assess whether the learner has the prerequisite skills necessary to be engaged in the current tutoring session. Depending on your content area, this will depend on how the warm-up may look for each learner. This warm-up should not take more than 10 minutes and should segue into the topic(s) that will be learned in the tutoring session.

Uploading Files in the Virtual Classroom

When it comes to uploading files, this can range from a warm-up activity, mini-assessments, or even a presentation that is used for the tutoring session. It's always a great idea to use visuals to help your learners with learning the material. Depending on the type of file that is being updated, it will determine the amount of time that will need to be spent performing this task. Just a heads up, some files can lock up the virtual classroom while loading so you do want to make sure that you arrive ahead of the tutoring session so that it will already be uploaded for future references in the tutoring session.

Checking the Virtual Classroom Settings

Another important task to check before the tutoring session is the virtual classroom settings, especially when it comes to audio and the microphone. Once the learner enters the tutoring session, you may have to ask him or her if they can hear you and vice versa. Once that is done, the tutoring session should be ready to begin without any concerns. It is wise to let the learner know that if either you or her gets kicked out of the virtual classroom that the expecta-tion is to log back in to continue the tutoring session. If that does happen, then this technical difficulty should not count towards the tutoring session time.

Let's look at a sample opening of an online tutoring session to see how this works together with the welcome message and so forth.

(Online Tutor Arrived 15 minutes early to the online tutoring session and typed the welcome message.)

**Online Tutor
[Mrs. Amaiya]:**

Welcome to Our Online Tutoring Session, Trinity!

Please take a moment and type both your first and last name.

Please solve the problem in the chat window. You can show your work on the whiteboard.

Look forward to working with you,
Your Favorite Online Tutor.

(Online Learner enters the classroom 15 minutes later; Online Learner types response in the chat OR speak to the online tutor using a microphone.)

**Online Learner
[Trinity]:**

Hi, Mrs. Amaiya. I will solve that problem right now. May I have a new whiteboard?

(Mrs. Amaiya writes the objectives for the tutoring session in both the chat and the whiteboard; she speaks to Trinity now about it.)

Mrs. Amaiya:

In today's session, we are going to solve word problems by using addition, subtraction, multiplication, and division. What are some problem solving strategies that you have used before?

Trinity:

Well, sometimes I draw a picture, but mostly I guess my answer after working the problem and eliminating answer choices.

Mrs. Amaiya:

Okay, thanks for being honest. Did you know that there are six different problem-solving strategies to use in math? Let's look at them on the whiteboard and we will watch a short video clip of how they are used when solving problems in the real world.

(The actual tutoring lesson begins.)

Expert's Advice: Mrs. Amaiya did a very good job of setting up her online tutoring session before the student arrived. As you can see, this is a lot of information to try to set up, and it will take about the first 15 minutes of a session to get started. Rather than take time away from the learner, I highly recommend that tutors arrive in their tutoring sessions at least 10-15 minutes before it starts. Also, during the tutoring session, Mrs. Amaiya could use both verbal and emoticons to show praise for Trinity's progress.

Now let's take a look at a sample closing of a tutoring session.

(Trinity took her mini-assessment, and now it is time to bring the session to a close in an organized fashion.)

Online Tutor
[Mrs. Amaiya]: In the chatbox, you should see a question that asks you to summarize what was learned today. Please type your response.

(Online Learner, Trinity, recalls the mini-assessment, which happened to be a math essay question. The math essay question was the following: Rayneisha is a new student in your class. She really does not understand how to solve triangles. How would you explain to Rayneisha how to classify triangles and find the area of triangles? Please show your work.)

Mrs. Amaiya: What did you learn today? Do you still have any questions? Are you sure?

Trinity: I learned how to solve word problems and classify triangles. No, I do not have any questions. I just got some make-up work that needs to be done at school.

| Mrs. Amaiya: | If you do not have any further questions, then this session has ended. See you next week, and it was a pleasure working with you. |
| Trinity: | Okay, Bye Mrs. Amaiya and thanks for your help. |

(The tutoring session ends and both Trinity and Mrs. Amaiya logs out of the virtual classroom.)

> **Expert's Advice:** Mrs. Amaiya allowed Trinity to ask any additional questions if she had any. It seems like Trinity passed her mini-assessment because Mrs. Amaiya did not take the time to discuss it at the close of the tutoring session. It could also mean that time was running out and the mini-assessment would need to be graded and it would be discussed at the next session. It is very unclear. However, this is a sample of how online tutoring sessions should be closed. The goal is not to re-introduce topics, but to get a good understanding of what was learned in the tutoring session and to provide an opportunity to the learner regarding additional topics that may need to be addressed at a future tutoring session. Most importantly, the student was able to reflect upon their learning.

Structure of Online Tutoring Sessions

A typical online tutoring session can last anywhere from 45 minutes to 120 minutes. Depending on the client's needs and attention span, it will determine the length of the tutoring session.

Here are suggested pacing schedules for a typical tutoring session ranging from 45 minutes to 120 minutes:

45-minutes Tutoring (Sessions	60-minutes Tutoring Sessions	90-minutes Tutoring Sessions	120-minutes Tutoring Sessions
• Open session (5 mins.) • Subject 1 (25 mins.) • Mini-Assessment (10 mins.) • Close Session (5 mins.)	• Open session (5 mins.) • Subject 1 (35 mins.) • Mini-Assessment (15 mins.) • Close Session (5 mins.)	• Open session (5 mins.) • Subject 1 (25 mins.) • Subject 2 (25 mins.) • Guided Practice (15 mins.) • Mini-Assessment (15 mins.) • Close Session (5 mins.)	• Open session (5 mins.) • Subject 1 (25 mins.) • Subject 2 (25 mins.) • Subject 3 (25 mins.) • Subject 4 (25 mins.) • Problem Solving (25 mins.) • Mini-Assessment (25 mins.) • Close Session (5 mins.)

Please keep in mind that all online tutoring sessions should be tailored to your client's needs. For instance, if you have a client with special needs, more time may be spent on one or two subjects, depending on his or her comfort level. In any event, these pacing schedules only serve as a starting point for structuring tutoring sessions.

Writing Monitoring Notes for Clients during Tutoring Sessions

Have you ever gone to your doctor several months after a visit? What happened? I am guessing that your doctor was able to recall the last session by looking at your chart. Did you know that he was looking at his notes in your file? The same process applies with your clients in your tutoring practice—you keep notes on your client's progress.

Monitoring notes serve three purposes:

1. They are used to help keep track of the client's progress.
2. They are used to help keep you fully informed about instructional decisions.
3. They are used to keep clients (and parents) informed of their (or their child's) progress. (Holland-Johnson, 2010, p. 92).

Whether you tutor face-to-face or online, it is best practice to keep monitoring notes on all clients as a way to provide data-driven tutoring services.

Components of Online Monitoring Notes

There are eight components that are useful for both the clients and tutors. These components are listed below:

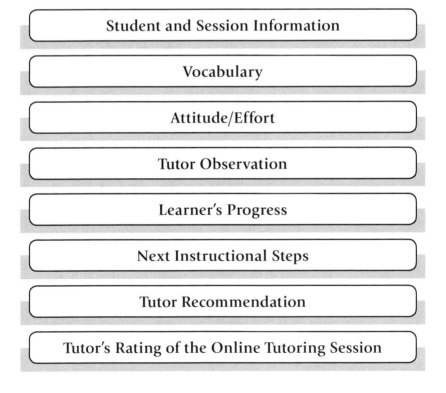

Student and Session Information

Vocabulary

Attitude/Effort

Tutor Observation

Learner's Progress

Next Instructional Steps

Tutor Recommendation

Tutor's Rating of the Online Tutoring Session

Student and Session Information

For every monitoring note, the tutor should be listed, along with the student who is being tutored. Other session information such as the date and time that the session takes place and the learning objective(s) slated for the tutoring session should be listed in this session as well.

Vocabulary

It is helpful to know the type of terminology that is being used in each tutoring session. This helps both the clients and tutors when it comes time to send out progress reports. Most importantly, this is a great way to show that grade level vocabulary is being used in tutoring sessions rather than slang for content-related vocabulary.

Attitude/Effort

The Attitude/Effort is considered nonacademic factors in tutoring sessions. However, this type of data offers vital information regarding the atmosphere of the tutoring session and how committed the learner was to the tutoring session. In other words, it helps to better understand why a learner made progress or not.

Tutor Observation

Tutor observations are the tutor's informal assessment of how the learner is performing in the session and how the content helped the student. This is another type of qualitative data that adds value to monitoring notes and hold tutor's accountable for their tutoring sessions.

Learner's Progress

This component will detail how the learner performed during the session.

"It should be in narrative form, but succinct, so that you are able to get an overall picture of the client's strengths and weaknesses during the session. If any mini-assessments are given at the end of the session, you should include the results. For example, a client named Shirley got three out of four test questions correct, which is 75 percent. As a result, Shirley has mastered how to compare fractions using concrete objects. A short paragraph (three to five sentences) should be included in this section for each subject that you are working on. For instance, if you are working on math and reading skills, there should be a section clearly labeled "Math and Reading," followed by the name of the activity or skill so that clients can understand the information. This is important because parents or guardians or adult clients are responsible for payment. Once this section has been completed, you should list the next instructional step(s)" (Holland-Johnson, 2010, p. 94).

Next Instructional Steps

This component is dedicated to determining the next instructional step. This is where information regarding how a learner has mastered a particular learning objective will come in handy. On the other hand, this is the section in which tutors should definitely document what are the next instructional steps for learners who did not master the content presented in the online tutoring session. This information is typically shared in progress reports that are sent out to clients and parents, if the clients are minors.

Tutor Recommendation

Since the tutor is working with the learner, it is very important to get their professional recommendation regarding the student's next step. This information is typically shared in progress reports that are sent out to clients and parents, if the clients are minors.

Tutor's Rating of the Online Tutoring Session

It is important to allow the tutor to rate the online tutoring session since students will have an opportunity to do the same thing. This is a great way to go back and look at the tutor's performance in the virtual classroom. In addition, this is a great way to find out about any technical difficulties whether it be on either the student's or tutor's computer. The bottom line is that it is documented in the monitoring notes if anything transpires.

Now that you have some strategies to help you with conducting quality online tutoring sessions, let your spirit guide you when you are starting and operating your online tutoring business.

Should you have questions or comments for me, suggestions for future material, or tips, feel free to email me at following: drhollandj@myonlinetutoringbusiness.com.

Join our Membership Group at www.myonlinetutoringbusiness.com to gain access to exclusive content and interact with Dr. Holland-Johnson so that you can strategically move your tutoring business from good to great.

Last but not least, if you are interested in networking with like-minded tutor business owners, join our FREE LinkedIn Group—My Online Tutoring Business.

Our LinkedIn Group is growing fast and group members are eager to connect with you and share their tutoring experiences with you. We truly have what you would call a Professional Learning Community.

Until next time, Happy Tutoring!

Reference

Holland-Johnson, A. (2010). *Becoming a better tutor: A data-driven approach to tutoring.* Bloomington, IN: iUniverse.

About the Author

D r. Alicia Holland-Johnson is one of those rare people who can say she is an educator, professional tutor, instructional designer, curriculum developer, online professor, life coach, consultant, speaker, and author and mean it.

She started her teaching career at the age of 20 and later earned her doctorate degree in Education from Nova Southeastern University in Ft. Lauderdale, Florida in 2010 at the age of 26.

Her global learning organization, iGlobal Educational Services LLC, has attracted clients such as school districts throughout the United States, and other leading organizations, including in the private sector.

Dr. Holland-Johnson consults with tutoring and other learning organizations both large and small. Her tutoring blog for tutors has been online since 2010 and has expanded her tutoring knowledge to an international consulting firm, *The Tutor Outreach Group.*

Typically, she speaks at major conferences each year on topics in education, including tutoring. Dr. Holland-Johnson is an online associate faculty member at Ashford University where she teaches both undergraduate and graduate courses in the School of Education.

Also, Dr. Holland-Johnson has held appointments as an adjunct online professor in the Graduate School of Education at both Capella University and American College of Education where she taught various courses in Education. At the American College of Education, Dr. Holland-Johnson also supervises adult learners in the Bilingual and English as a Second Language (ESL) Internship

Program. Lastly, she teaches strategies for student success and critical thinking courses at Everest Online.

When Dr. Holland-Johnson is not developing new content, tutoring, teaching, or consulting with her clients, you can usually find her sight-seeing and spending quality time with her family.

You can also find more of her work at www.drholland-johnson.com. If you are interested in working with Dr. Holland-Johnson, please contact her using the contact form at her website.

Index

H

I

L

M

N

O

Made in the USA
San Bernardino, CA
04 June 2014